DANGEROUS JOBS

COAST GUARD RESCUE SWIMMER

BY NICK GORDON

BELLWETHER MEDIA · MINNEAPOLIS, MN

Are you ready to take it to the extreme? Torque books thrust you into the action-packed world of sports, vehicles, mystery, and adventure. These books may include dirt, smoke, fire, and dangerous stunts.
WARNING: read at your own risk.

Library of Congress Cataloging-in-Publication Data

Gordon, Nick.
Coast Guard rescue swimmer / by Nick Gordon.
p. cm. -- (Torque: Dangerous jobs)
Includes bibliographical references and index.
Summary: "Engaging images accompany information about Coast Guard rescue swimmers. The combination of high-interest subject matter and light text is intended for students in grades 3 through 7" --Provided by publisher.
Audience: Grades 3-7.
ISBN 978-1-60014-778-4 (hbk. : alk. paper)
1. United States. Coast Guard--Search and rescue operations--Juvenile literature. 2. Lifesaving--Juvenile literature. 3. Lifesaving--Vocational guidance--Juvenile literature. I. Title.
VG53.G68 2013
363.28'6--dc23 2012004403

This edition first published in 2013 by Bellwether Media, Inc.

Printed in the United States of America, North Mankato, MN.

TABLE OF CONTENTS

CHAPTER 1

RESCUE AT SEA

Waves crash against a small lifeboat. A storm is building. A man clings to his life vest as the boat fills with water and begins to sink. Suddenly he hears the sound of a Jayhawk helicopter. A rescue swimmer from the United States Coast Guard is on her way!

6003
ARD
03

A Select Group

Only around 300 rescue swimmers serve in the U.S. Coast Guard.

The helicopter hovers near the lifeboat. The rescue swimmer jumps into the cold, choppy ocean. She rushes to help the man keep his head above water. She attaches him to a **harness** and signals the helicopter. It lifts him to safety. The rescue swimmer has saved another life.

CHAPTER 2

COAST GUARD RESCUE SWIMMERS

Rescue swimmers are some of the toughest members of the U.S. Coast Guard. Their job is to rescue people who are **stranded** at sea, on cliffs, or in caves. The rescues often take place during storms with strong winds and huge waves.

6581
COAST GUARD

It takes a lot of hard work to become a rescue swimmer. **Trainees** go to the Aviation Technical Training Center in North Carolina. There they must pass difficult fitness tests. They need to become strong, fast swimmers. They also need to be experts at jumping from helicopters. Only about half of all trainees graduate.

Keeping Fit

Every month, rescue swimmers must pass the physical tests required for their work.

Push-ups	50 (2-minute time limit)
Sit-ups	60 (2-minute time limit)
Pull-ups	5 (no time limit)
Chin-ups	5 (no time limit)
Crawl Swim	500 yards (12-minute time limit)
Underwater Swim	25 yards (repeat 4 times, 60 seconds apart)
Buddy Tow	200 yards

Rescue swimmers often give medical care to the people they rescue. Trainees learn how to give **first aid** at the Coast Guard Training Center in California. Every trainee becomes a skilled **emergency medical technician (EMT)**.

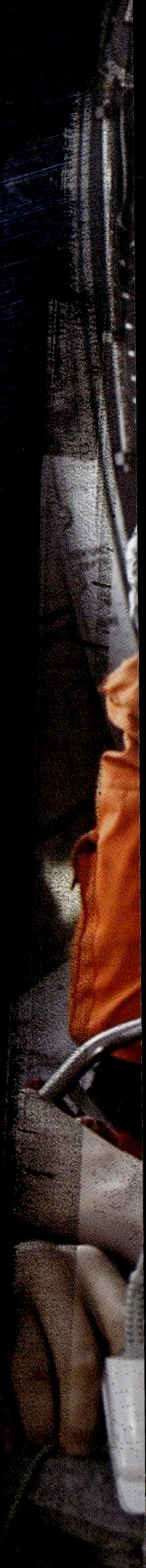

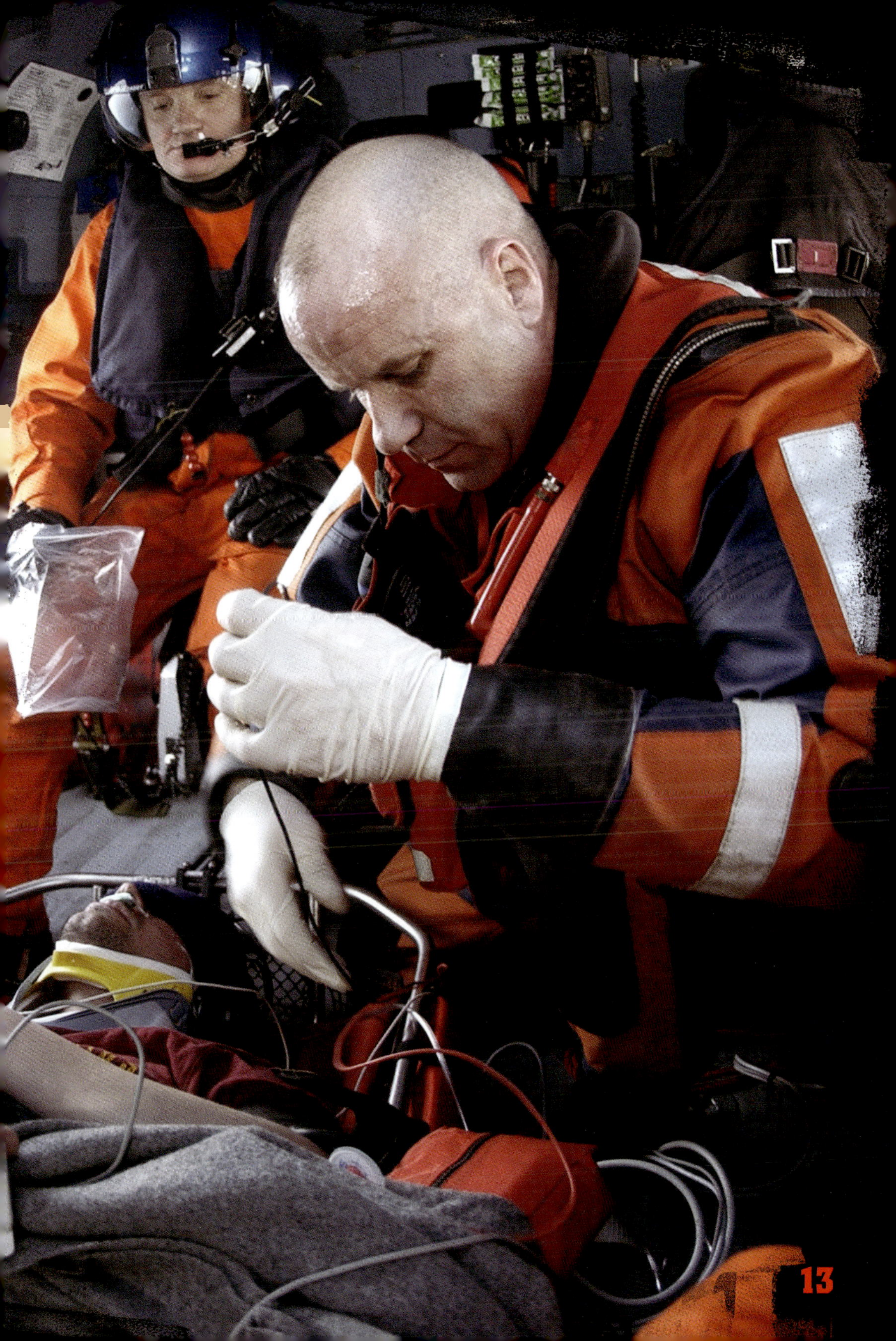

All Tied Up

Rescue swimmers often rescue pilots forced to eject from their planes. The pilots often get tangled in parachute lines. Rescue swimmers learn to untangle these lines.

Rescue swimmers also spend five days at the Advanced Helicopter Rescue School in Oregon. There they practice their skills in extreme conditions. They test their ability to fight massive waves for 30 minutes. They **rappel** down cliffs and swim into caves. This hands-on training helps prepare them for real rescues.

Rescue swimmers need gear to stay safe. They wear **dry suits** and gloves to stay warm and dry. **Fins** help them move in choppy water. Masks and **snorkels** help them see and breathe. Rescue swimmers also wear harnesses. They connect to lines that lift them and the **victims** to safety.

CHAPTER 3

DANGER!

Coast Guard rescue swimmers risk their lives every time they respond to a call. Swimmers sometimes have to jump more than 30 feet (9 meters) to reach the water. This drop can cause severe bruising. It can even knock someone out. Rescue swimmers often enter waters that are extremely cold or rough. Swimmers must remain calm and focused.

U.S.
COAST GUA D
6039

Always On Call

Coast Guard rescue swimmers take turns working 24-hour shifts. They must be ready to respond to a call at any moment while on duty.

Victims can also be a threat to rescue swimmers. People who are drowning often panic. They may grab at a rescue swimmer and drag him or her underwater. Sometimes rescue swimmers must avoid the **debris** of ships or aircraft. Their training prepares them for the worst. Rescue swimmers take the leap no matter the risk.

Tragedy on the Job

On June 8, 1997, rescue swimmer James G. Caines and three other Coast Guard members died. They were preparing for a rescue when their helicopter crashed into the sea. It was Caines' first mission as a rescue swimmer.

Glossary

debris—the remains of something that has been destroyed

dry suits—body suits that keep swimmers warm and dry in cold waters

emergency medical technician (EMT)—someone trained to give basic medical care to a person on the way to a hospital

fins—flat rubber shoes with paddle-like extensions

first aid—emergency medical care given to a sick or injured person before he or she reaches a hospital

harness—straps that attach someone to a rope or line

rappel—to descend while attached to a rope

snorkels—tubes that allow rescue swimmers to breathe underwater; one end of a snorkel goes into a rescue swimmer's mouth and the other end stays above the surface.

stranded—stuck in a particular place with no way to escape

trainees—people training for a job

victims—people who are hurt, killed, or made to suffer

To Learn More

AT THE LIBRARY

David, Jack. *United States Coast Guard*. Minneapolis, Minn.: Bellwether Media, 2008.

La Bella, Laura. *Search and Rescue Swimmers*. New York, N.Y.: Rosen Pub., 2009.

Reeves, Diane Lindsey. *Scary Jobs*. New York, N.Y.: Ferguson, 2009.

ON THE WEB

Learning more about Coast Guard rescue swimmers is as easy as 1, 2, 3.

1. Go to www.factsurfer.com.

2. Enter "Coast Guard rescue swimmers" into the search box.

3. Click the "Surf" button and you will see a list of related Web sites.

With factsurfer.com, finding more information is just a click away.

Index